AUBREY BURL

PREHISTORIC STONE CIRCLES

CIRCLES

Fourth edition

SHIRE ARCHAEOLOGY

Cover photograph
Castlerigg stone circle. Reproduced by kind permission of Adele Pescod.

British Library Cataloguing in Publication Data:
Burl, Aubrey
Prehistoric stone circles. – 4th ed. – (Shire archaeology; 9)
1. Stone circles – Great Britain
I. Title
936.1'01
ISBN-10: 0 7478 0609 8.

Published in 2010 by
SHIRE PUBLICATIONS LTD
Midland House, West Way, Botley, Oxford OX2 0PH, UK.
(Website: www.shirebooks.co.uk)

Series Editor: James Dyer.

ISBN-13: 978 0 74780 609 7.

Number 9 in the Shire Archaeology series.

First published 1979. Second edition 1983. Expanded third edition 1988; reprinted 1991, 1994 and, with amendments, 1997 and 2001. Fourth edition, with new text and illustrated in colour, 2005; reprinted 2010.

Printed in China through Worldprint Ltd.

Contents

Glossary

Archaeo-astronomy: the study of astronomical practices among ancient societies. When investigating pre-literate communities such as those of prehistoric Britain and Ireland, where there are no written records, such research is exceptionally difficult.

Barrow: an artificial mound of earth, chalk or turf used to cover one or more burials.

Beaker people: continental people who first entered Britain around 2600 BC, their name coming from their distinctive and elegant pots, often buried with the dead under round barrows. They may have been the first metal-users in Britain.

Beltane: an Iron Age festival to celebrate the coming of spring and held on the night before 1st May. Associated with the lighting of fires, it may have originated in the Neolithic period.

Bluestones: the name given to the mixture of stones, mainly of dolerite, probably from the Preseli mountains of Pembrokeshire, used in the second phase of Stonehenge.

Boulder-grave: a burial place of large stones, consisting of several low ones embedded in the ground and supporting a heavy capstone. Such monuments are quite often found with the multiple (recumbent) stone circles in south-west Ireland.

Cairn: an artificial mound of smallish stones covering one or more burials.

Chambered tomb: at first a burial place, later a shrine, of the Neolithic period. It consisted of a stone-built passage giving access to one or several chambers. It could be covered by a long or round barrow or cairn.

Circle-henge: a henge whose central plateau supported a stone circle.

Cist: a grave lined with thin slabs of stone and covered by a capstone. Cists were sometimes inserted inside existing stone circles.

Concentric circle: a stone circle with another inside it. Usually the inner ring was of taller stones. Never numerous, such rings were built in south-west Scotland, Ireland and Wessex.

Cove: three standing stones, one at the back, two at the sides, like an unroofed sentry-box. There may once have been a fourth lying in front of them.

Cromlech: a non-circular ring of standing stones in Brittany, most common in the Morbihan.

Embanked circle: a stone circle whose pillars were embedded in a bank of stones or earth. They were common in the Peak District, and there were others in Yorkshire and Wales.

Fer-à-cheval: a horseshoe-shaped setting of standing stones, most common in Brittany.

Five-stone ring: a *four-poster* with a fifth stone prostrate in its western quadrant. Such rings exist almost exclusively in south-west Ireland.

Four-poster: four stones apparently standing at the corners of a small, crude rectangle but actually set on a circle. Most commonly found in central Scotland.

Gnomon: a standing stone for astronomical observations. Originally it was a pillar whose shadow indicated the time of day. Sundials have gnomons.

Henge: a circular or oval earthwork of the late Neolithic and early Bronze Age. It had a ditch and bank of earth, chalk or gravel with one or more entrances, and it surrounded an open central space.

Kerbstones: heavy stones, side by side, around the base of a *barrow*, *cairn* or *chambered tomb*.

Lintel: a stone across the top of two uprights like those on the sarsen circle and the trilithons at Stonehenge.

Megalithic: of very large stones.

Monolith: a single standing stone.

Passage-tomb: a round chambered tomb with a passage leading to a burial chamber, common in Ireland and Scotland.

Recumbent stone circle: a circle whose stones rose in height towards the south, where a heavy block lay prostrate anywhere from SSE to south-west between two tall flanking pillars. Most numerous in north-east Scotland, there were variant forms in south-west Ireland.

Ring-cairn: a low round *cairn* without a passage but with an open central space in which cremated bones were often placed. Ring-cairns also occur inside *recumbent stone circles* in north-east Scotland and the Clava Cairns of Inverness-shire.

Wessex: the area of southern England including all or parts of Wiltshire, Dorset, Berkshire, Somerset and Hampshire, which supported a large prehistoric population on the easily worked chalk soils.

1
Introduction

Whether in northern Scotland, standing in the moorland hollow where the stones of Guidebest curve alongside the Latheronwheel river, or looking at the desolate ring of Tregeseal 600 miles (965 km) to the south among the tors of Land's End, one senses an emptiness about these ancient ruins. It comes from the realisation of how ignorant we are about the people who raised the stones. 'There are no remembrances of the founders, any other than an uninterrupted tradition of their being sacred', wrote William Stukeley, one of the first chroniclers of these rings. Almost three centuries later his words are still true. What knowledge we have about the circles comes from the work of archaeologists with considerable assistance from geologists, astronomers and statisticians.

Amongst the research there has sometimes been an overemphasis on the significance of Stonehenge, which is only one of many more than a thousand stone circles and the most uncharacteristic of all of them. Once again Stukeley had a better perspective:

> Tho' Stonehenge be the proudest singularity of this sort ... yet there are so many others, manifestly form'd upon the same, or kindred design, by the same measure, and for the same purpose, all over the Britannic isles, that we can have no room to doubt of their being made by the same people, and that by direction of the British Druids.

1. Tregeseal, Land's End, Cornwall.

2. A general view of Stonehenge, Wiltshire, from the north-east.

Druids excepted, for they had nothing to do with the building and use of stone circles, it has taken a long time to add much to Stukeley's observations. Stone circles are among the most fascinating and enigmatic of our prehistoric monuments, yet little was known about them until the twentieth century. Now we do have a good idea of when they were put up, in which parts of Britain, how they were erected, what their origins were, and what is likely to be found in them.

What they were used for is a different question. The answer will probably always be elusive and for the present we must be content with guesses based on the architecture and contents of these weathered sites, whose survival for so many centuries is itself a matter of marvel.

Since the late twentieth century much has been written about the theoretical measurements, geometry and astronomy of megalithic rings, as well as about the symbolism of their architecture. Whereas the possibility of a ring being an observatory is a matter of conjecture, the presence of human cremations is not. Nor is the choice of stones, their selected shapes, their chosen colours, or the frustratingly uninformative carvings that tantalise in a few circles such as Long Meg and Her Daughters in Cumbria.

The rings were not erected in a haphazard plan, nor were their stones casually discovered. Each was part of an intended design. The materials and structure of a circle were as significant to their builders as the nave, choir, altar, misericords and gargoyles were to the masons, carpenters and priests of a Christian church. But the builders of stone circles were illiterate. They left no bible except for the stones themselves.

2
The origins of stone circles

Where or why the first stone circle was built is unknown. At one time, because of the scraps of decorated beaker pottery discovered in well-known but completely unrepresentative circles such as Avebury and Stonehenge, it was believed that megalithic rings had been constructed by Beaker people during the Bronze Age. The evidence deceived. The earliest circles were the work of native farming communities of the late fourth millennium BC at a time in the Neolithic or New Stone Age many centuries before continental Beaker people entered Britain.

The rings were built where stone was freely available, not in the fertile lowlands but in the west on the hillsides and among the mountains of England, Wales and Scotland. They began with a change in the weather.

For as long as men could remember, and their fathers, and their fathers before them, the weather had been bad, with long periods of rain, dark clouds, cold and winds blowing across desolate fields. Crops would not ripen. Cattle sickened. It was as though the skies were angry.

It is believed that the catastrophe was the result of a volcanic eruption in Greenland, but, whatever the cause, its effects were felt all over northern Europe and were disastrous for the inhabitants of Britain and Ireland. Helpless in a seemingly never-ending calamity, they turned away from the ancestors they believed had once protected them and, instead, looked to the threatening skies. Stone circles were born of desperation.

People pleaded with those skies, hoping to calm them. Old burial places, where the bones of their once-powerful forefathers lay, were abandoned. Open-air rings were put up, of earth in the east of Britain, where there was no stone, of posts in woodland areas, of stone in the west, where thousands of boulders lay exposed on the hills. Some centuries before 3000 BC the first circles of stone were raised, some in the north-west of Ireland, others in western Britain, in the Lake District of England and along the Atlantic coasts of Scotland. In these unroofed enclosures people looked to the heavens, certain that the rings protected people inside them, that even strangers were safe. These were places beyond the ordinary world. They were sanctuaries.

It may have been from about 3300 BC that the very first great megalithic rings and henges were erected. As yet, the earliest carbon-14 assay from a stone circle comes from the Lochmaben Stone near Gretna Green, dated to 2525±150 bc, a period between 3350 BC and 2950 BC. It was contemporary with some of the first henges built in lowland Britain: Llandegai by the Menai Straits, around 3250 BC; Arminghall in Norfolk, whose inner horseshoe setting of posts was dated to 2490±150 bc (c.3230

3. Lochmaben Stone, Dumfries-shire, with the Solway Firth and the Cumbrian mountains in the background.

BC); and Barford in the woodlands of Warwickshire, put up around 3110 BC (2416±64 bc). These free-standing earthworks, 30 metres or more in diameter, may have derived from earlier Neolithic round funerary enclosures with their now-outmoded burial mounds. Stone circles were probably the counterparts of henges in those highland areas where it was hard to dig but where building stone was plentiful.

Their origins differed. Near Sligo in the north-western corner of Ireland circles developed from heavy banks of stones surrounding tombs. In Britain the first rings may have been imitations of the unroofed eastern henges whose circular banks of soil and turf were broken by one or more entrances.

More than a thousand stone circles still exist, some damaged almost beyond recognition. A catalogue compiled in 2000 listed more than 1300 sites, several discovered in modern times. On the island of Arran a peat-covered, unconsidered stone circle was found on Machrie Moor in 1978. A thousand is a conservative figure and perhaps represents only half of the original number. The rings were put up over some fifteen hundred

4. Machrie Moor XI, Arran, during the rain-affected excavation.

years within an area stretching 800 miles (1300 km) from Shetland down to Cornwall and 400 miles (650 km) from Aberdeenshire across to western Ireland.

Over so many centuries and inside 300,000 square miles (777,000 square km) no uniform pattern of architecture or custom could be expected and, undoubtedly, the rites inside the first rings were very different from those in the last.

3
Early stone circles:
late Neolithic age, *c*.3650 to 2900 BC

The very earliest stone circles in the British Isles may be in the north-west of Ireland. In the Carrowmore cemetery of County Sligo are 'boulder-circles', open rings of high boulders, shoulder to shoulder, enclosing burial cairns. They are a transitional form of monument between encircled passage-tombs and the true stone circle.

Of the five great Irish passage-tomb cemeteries from the Boyne group in the east to Carrowkeel and Carrowmore in the west four are similar. The exception is Carrowmore. Early Ordnance Survey surveyors were percipient, astutely labelling its unusual rings as 'Stone Circles' on their maps. Many of the so-called kerbed cairns and chambered tombs in this poorly protected cemetery are embryonic rings, forms imitating the heavy kerbs of cairns, and they were ancestral to the true free-standing stone circle.

In plan Carrowmore could be likened to a city with suburbs and surrounding villages. The 'city's' centre is the Neolithic chambered tomb known as Listoghil, Site 51. Surrounding it at a distance are the 'suburbs' of boulder-circles along the edge of a buckled oval about 750 by 500 metres. Over the centuries some have been robbed, many demolished, as convenient material for walls, doorways and roads. The outlying 'villages' are the true stone circles lying in a broken line to the north.

A score of the megalithic 'mongrels' known as boulder-circles survives. They are rings of tall, closely set boulders that act as walls for flat-topped burial cairns. If seen from the air they would resemble a bicycle wheel, the narrow tyre, the long spokes and the hub. The 'tyre' was the enclosing bank of high boulders; the 'spokes' were the inner cairn of smaller stones and the 'hub' was a place of burial – a small megalithic tomb, or a cist, or a grave.

The twenty-eight stones of the first boulder-circle, Site 4, stand in a large oval. It provided a C-14 assay of 2370±75 bc, *c*.3150–2950 BC. The ring is at the beginning of a line of increasingly spaced, ever-mutating monuments extending to the NNE for almost three-quarters of a mile (just over 1 km), by the end of which the sites had become true stone circles.

Just to its ESE is a ring of thirty-three heavy boulders. It is a big site with massive stones weighing 4 to 5 tons each. It would have taken perhaps a score of workers to move them into position. The interior is, as usual, a platform of cobbles.

Figure 1. Possible circles of the early period. 1 Ballynoe, County Down (J 481404). 2 Brats Hill, Cumbria (NY 173023). 3 Castlerigg, Cumbria (NY 292236). 4 Lochmaben Stone, Dumfries-shire (NY 312659). 5 Long Meg and Her Daughters, Cumbria (NY 571373). 6 Stones of Stenness, Orkney (HY 306125). 7 Swinside, Cumbria (SD 172883). 8 Carrowmore, County Sligo (centred on G 663335).

5. Carrowmore boulder-circle, County Sligo.

Well to the north is another, an open ring, with only eight of its exceptionally big and well-spaced stones surviving but with no trace of a platform cairn against which the stones could have stood. In any other county or country this setting would be recognised as a stone circle. Another free-standing ring, Site 9, still has eight of its enormous, well-spaced stones. There is a huge block at the south-west but no trace of an

6. Carrowmore stone circle.

maybe dating from before 3000 BC.

Its stones range in height, the tallest at the WSW shaped like a grazing mammoth. Across the circle it faces a triangular slab whose inner face is decorated with forty-three or more cupmarks. Altogether four, maybe five, stones of the ring have carvings: an outlier to the south-east, stones at the north-east, north-west and NNE, and a doubtful pillar at the south-west.

The ring is perhaps the most intriguing 'astronomical' site in the north of Ireland. The enthusiastic archaeo-astronomer Boyle Somerville suggested that there was a fine alignment from the great pillar at the south-west to the cupmarked stone. Although 1.2 metres wide, this triangular stone has a sharply peaked top that defines the sightline neatly, leading the eye to the small but conspicuous hill-summit of Tullyrap 5 miles (8 km) away, above which the sun rose in early May. 'The azimuth of this line, in any case, is precisely that of sunrise on Bealltaine [6th May]; and it is important to note that the present name, "Beltany Hill", gives the almost exact pronunciation of the Gaelic name of this "May Day" celebration. This seems a very convincing proof of the connexion of the Circle with the date found by orientation.'

If Beltany Tops was indeed a ring derived from the Carrowmore tradition it had no apparent partners anywhere in the north of Ireland. As in other regions where there was an innovative stone circle, the creation of others may have been hindered, evenly physically discouraged and resisted by native users of chambered tombs just to the east. Beltany may have been the finest but the last of its line. A longer-lasting tradition exists in Britain.

Concentrating around the coasts of the Irish Sea and the Atlantic sea route from Ireland to Scotland, the early British circles were few but

10. Castlerigg, Cumbria. The two tall stones form the entrance at the north.

impressive. They were large, usually over 30.5 metres in diameter, and were true circles although some had a flattened arc, perhaps because of the custom of several work gangs putting up separate sections of the circumference. Some, such as Swinside and Castlerigg, had well-defined entrances. From these earliest circles oval shapes may have developed in southern Scotland.

Few finds have come from these rings – just occasional bits of Neolithic pottery and some stone axes – and the only radiocarbon dates yet available are from the Lochmaben Stone, Dumfries-shire, with a midpoint of 3150 BC, and from the Stones of Stenness in Orkney, where two determinations averaged 2297 bc (*c*.2965 BC). As the Lochmaben Stone, now one tumbled boulder but originally a spacious oval 55 by 46 metres, is on the other side of the Solway Firth from the Lake District it is arguable that some of the rings there were even earlier, maybe erected before 3200 BC.

The situation of the rings around the mountains of the Lake District suggests they were the creations of people engaged in the prospecting and manufacture of valuable stone axes during the middle and late Neolithic periods, just as some Yorkshire henges are believed to have been the depots from which axes were redistributed to Wessex and other regions of dense population.

Many of the rings, for example Castlerigg and Swinside in Cumbria and Ballynoe in County Down, have closely set stones, very similar to the continuous banks of henges and, like them, broken by a conspicuous entrance, which in the case of the circles was defined by two pairs of stones or taller pillars. All of them were built of local stone dragged to the site by men and women. It is possible that oxen, castrated bulls,

11. Swinside, Cumbria.

12. The decorated outlier at Long Meg, Cumbria.

were used to move the stones from their source but there is no proof.

As well as Ballynoe in Ireland, the Rollright Stones in Oxfordshire have very similar architecture to that of Swinside in size, number of stones and entrance and may have been one of several staging posts for the sending of axes from Cumbria to southern England.

Outside some of the early circles stood isolated monoliths. Some of these outliers may have been erected in line with celestial events such as midsummer sunrise or midwinter sunset, as seems to be the case with the decorated outlier at Long Meg and Her Daughters near Penrith, but many of the outlying stones, such as those at Ballynoe, are too low for observations of the sky. Others, including the plough-scratched stone at Castlerigg near Keswick, have been moved from their original positions and do not provide reliable clues as to their intended function.

Stenness had an external holed stone that has been associated with fertility rites. Young couples betrothed themselves by clasping hands through the aperture.

It is probable that prehistoric societies, much concerned with death and fertility, incorporated sightlines to the sun or moon in the design of their ritual monuments by raising such gnomonic pillars. Symbolism rather than science, however, seems to have been the motive for such orientations. These early stone circles were never designed as refined observatories and their contents of human bone indicate the dedicatory, maybe even sacrificial, nature of the rites that went on in them.

Their open interiors, their low-lying positions, often in valleys and near rivers or lakes, and their great size all suggest that they were intended as gathering places for large groups. What the ceremonies were is impossible to know, especially as so few objects have been recovered. Yet, quite consistently, traces of fire and of human bone have been found – not complete skeletons but cremated pockets of bone, as though such relics were vital dedications when the stones were erected. A widespread form of ancestral cult may be suspected.

At Stenness the remains of a wooden mortuary building lay inside the ring, connected by rough paving to a central 'hearth' in which there were flecks of seaweed, broken pottery and burnt human bones.

Charcoal was discovered at Castlerigg, and also at Swinside accompanied by a 'minute fragment of human bone'. Several patches of

13. The 'outlier' at Castlerigg, Cumbria.

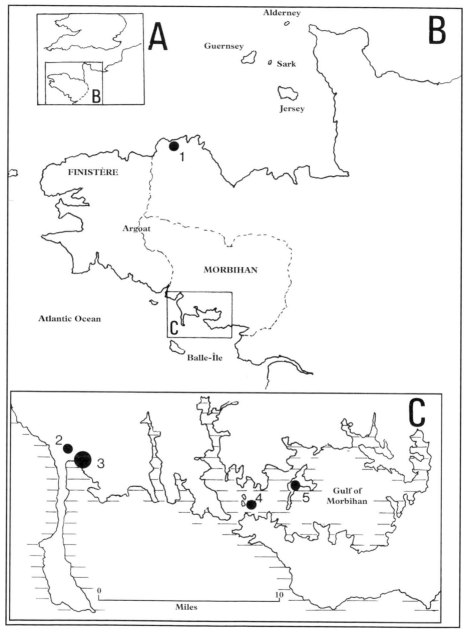

Figure 2. The megalithic enclosures of Brittany. 1 Tossen-Keler. 2 Crucuno. 3 Carnac: Ménec, Kermario, Kerlescan. 4 Er-Lannic. 5 Kergonan, Île-aux-Moines.

16. Ménec West, Carnac, Morbihan, Brittany, showing arcs of the cromlech's closely set stones around the intrusive houses.

There is support for the belief that such spacious rings continued in use for centuries. At Ménec West there had been a short avenue leading to the enclosure. Over the decades extensions were added to it section by section, as at Avebury's Kennet Avenue, whose sections were ultimately linked to a second avenue leading to the Sanctuary. In the same manner the two sides of the avenue at Ménec West were joined to the avenue of the even bigger cromlech of Ménec East almost half a mile (800 metres) away. Yet although the slightly zigzagged avenues were complete the custom of introducing more stones continued over the centuries, villagers erecting them one by one, year by year, in meaningless lines on either side of the avenues, eventually leading to the modern-day chaos of eleven or more raggedly twisting rows that leave bewildered visitors trying to understand the logic of their design.

There is no logic, just habit. In the early nineteenth century the antiquarian Cambry was told that even in his day, every year in June, a further stone was put up. In 1825 the Abbé Mahé received similar information: in an annual festival a midsummer fire burned on the Carnac Mound of the adjacent Tumulus Saint-Michel.

The reason for the ovoid rather than round shape of the cromlechs was probably astronomical, with the long and short axes, unavailable in a

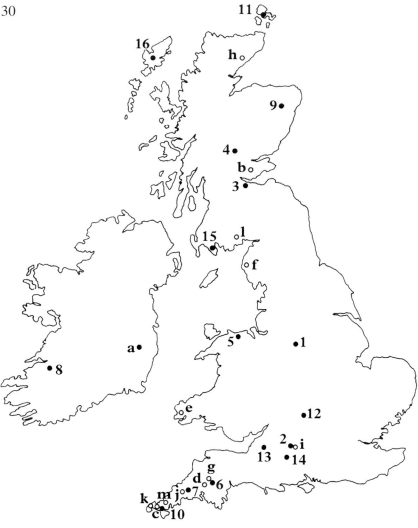

Figure 3. Possible circles of the middle period. Solid rings stand for sites worth visiting. Lettered rings represent other circles mentioned in the text. 1 Arbor Low, Derbyshire (SK 160636). 2 Avebury, Wiltshire (SU 103700). 3 Cairnpapple, West Lothian (NS 987717). 4 Croft Moraig, Perthshire (NN 797472). 5 Druid's Circle, Conwy (SH 722746). 6 Fernworthy, Devon (SX 655841). 7 Hurlers, Cornwall (SX 258714). 8 Grange, County Limerick (R 640410). 9 Loanhead of Daviot, Aberdeenshire (NJ 747288). 10 Merry Maidens, Cornwall (SW 432245). 11 Ring of Brodgar, Orkney (HY 294132). 12 Rollright Stones, Oxfordshire (SP 296308). 13 Stanton Drew, Somerset (ST 603630). 14 Stonehenge, Wiltshire (SU 123422). 15 Torhousekie, Wigtownshire (NX 383565). 16. Callanish, Lewis (NB 213330). a Athgreany, County Wicklow. b Balfarg, Fife. c Boscawen-Un, Cornwall. d Brisworthy, Devon. e Gors Fawr, Pembrokeshire. f Grey Croft, Cumbria. g Grey Wethers, Devon. h Guidebest, Caithness. i Sanctuary, Wiltshire. j Stripple Stones, Cornwall. k Tregeseal, Cornwall. l Twelve Apostles, Dumfries-shire. m Wendron, Cornwall.

21. The south-western arc of the great Outer Circle at Avebury, Wiltshire.

22. The Ring of Brodgar, Orkney.

26. Gors Fawr, Pembrokeshire. The Preseli mountains, the supposed source of the Stonehenge bluestones, rise behind the stone circle.

attractive uplands of forest and blanket bog.

Here and elsewhere in the south-west peninsula there were paired and treble rings: the Grey Wethers in Devon; the Hurlers, Wendron and Tregeseal in Cornwall. The multiple rings of Stanton Drew and Avebury may have belonged to the same tradition, circle added to circle over the years but seldom identical to those before it.

Other stone circles in Cornwall had centre stones, such as that at Boscawen-Un. From about 2400 BC avenues of stones led up to some rings along the Welsh Marches and in the southern foothills of Cumbria. Occasional concentric circles, maybe imitating wooden huts, were erected

27. The restored pair of stone circles at Grey Wethers, Dartmoor, Devon.

in Wessex and south-west Scotland.

Once disparagingly dismissed as 'rude stone monuments', many of these rings were in reality marvels of careful construction with sightlines built into them and were also monuments of several phases with as long as a thousand years between the first phase and the last. The wonderful site of Callanish on Lewis in the Outer Hebrides is an ideal example. It began as just a single 5 metre high stone near the coast, erected as a landmark for seamen. Some decades or even centuries later an oval about 13 by 12 metres was built around it. Six radiocarbon assays suggest a period between 2800 and 2700 BC.

Four centuries later a long avenue was laid out from the NNE that was aligned on the most southerly setting of the moon. More change followed. Three short single rows were added – one to the south, another westwards, a third at ENE. Each one was astronomical. The southern was aligned on the meridian, the western to the equinoctial sunset and the ENE directed to the rising of the galactic cluster of the Pleiades, the lovely Seven Sisters, around 1600 BC. Finally, almost in desecration, an insignificant little chambered tomb was crammed inside the ring.

It is all there in the stones. The messages were deciphered only in modern times, which is ironic because Callanish had been visited over two thousand years earlier, in around 300 BC, by the Greek explorer Pytheas. Later records imply that he called the ring a 'spherical temple' and learned that the moon visited it every nineteen years, the lunar cycle of 18.61 years. Folk memories are not always myths. The 'temple' has often mistakenly been identified as Stonehenge. The latitude of that great ring on Salisbury Plain is 500 miles (800 km) too far south for the moon to have behaved as Pytheas described.

28. The circle, rows and avenue at Callanish, Lewis, Outer Hebrides. A tiny passage-tomb lies just to the right of the centre stone.

31. The recumbent stone at Aikey Brae, Aberdeenshire. The spirit-level proved that the slab was exactly horizontal.

alignments and the deposits of cremated bone reveal that whatever occurred in these rings was probably derived from Neolithic burial customs. Similarly, it is possible that in the south the three-sided settings of stones known as 'coves' were symbolic representations of megalithic tomb entrances. Versions survive at Avebury, at Stanton Drew by the church, and, collapsed, inside Arbor Low. Even into the Bronze Age human bones may have been brought to them in the expectation that ancestral spirits could be conjured to the assistance of the living.

32. The recumbent stone circle at Loanhead of Daviot, Aberdeenshire. To its right are the remains of an enclosed cremation cemetery.

6
Late stone circles: early to middle Bronze Age, *c*.2200–1500 BC

It was probably during this final period that the majority of stone circles were erected, cramped rings of varying shapes, installed in regions of marginal soils: on the uplands of Dartmoor; the Peak District; in Ulster and south-west Ireland; in the hills of southern and northern Scotland; and around the fringes of the Welsh mountains. One very important group is to be found by Loch Roag on Lewis in the Western Isles.

Ovals predominate but the sites are so small – rarely exceeding 18 metres – that frequently it is difficult to decide whether one is surveying a good oval or a poor circle. Many of the sites were so close together that both their size and their proximity suggest that they were the creations of individual families. The weight of the stones does not contradict this. Few of them are megalithic and most could easily have been raised by a few men and women.

Each region had its own character. In northern Scotland rings were rare but instead there were multiple rows of tiny stones climbing uphill towards round cairns. In central Scotland ovals of six or eight stones intermingled with diminutive rectangles known as 'four-posters', which almost invariably contained an urned cremation. One four-poster at Ferntower is preserved on a golf-course. Another oddly situated ring is the survivor of a graded pair at Sandy Road, Perth, imprisoned in

33. Sandy Road stone circle, Perthshire. It is the survivor of a pair of rings and is now enclosed in a housing estate.

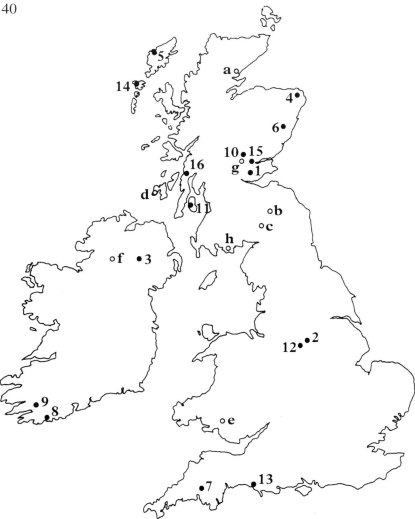

Figure 4. Possible circles of the late period. Solid rings stand for sites worth visiting. Open rings represent other circles mentioned in the text.
1 Balbirnie, Fife (NO 285030). 2 Barbrook II, Derbyshire (SK 277758). 3 Beaghmore, County Tyrone (H 685842). 4 Berrybrae, Aberdeenshire (NK 028572). 5 Loch Roag, Lewis (NB 2132). 6 Cullerlie, Aberdeenshire (NJ 785043). 7 Down Tor, Devon (SX 587694). 8 Drombeg, County Cork (W 247352). 9 Kealkil, County Cork (W 054556). 10 Lundin Farm, Perthshire (NN 882505). 11 Machrie Moor, Arran (NR 911324). 12 Nine Ladies, Derbyshire (SK 247634). 13 Nine Stones, Dorset (SY 611904). 14 Pobull Fhinn, North Uist (NF 844650). 15 Sandy Road, Perth (NO 132265). 16 Temple Wood, Argyll (NR 826979). a Aberscross, Sutherland. b Borrowston Rigg, Berwickshire. c Burgh Hill, Roxburghshire. d Cultoon, Islay. e Cerrig Duon, Powys. f Drumskinny, County Fermanagh. g Ferntower, Perthshire. h Glenquickan, Kirkcudbrightshire.

Graystones Close with modern houses around it. From it came a cremation and a late date for any stone circle of 1200±150 bc, an unhelpful date of between 1500 and 1250 BC. The cremation itself must be a warning. Such intrusive burials could have been inserted into a circle abandoned many years earlier.

Other rings of stone, hardly to be seen in the wiry grass, rest in the hills of the Cheviots. Circles with stones set in a rubble bank are numerous in the Peak District, most of their inconspicuous cairns robbed of their bones. On Dartmoor even smaller circles surrounded cairns approached by disproportionately long rows of stones. These cairns also have been dug into and their cists emptied but only a few flint arrowheads and bits of pot have reached the museums of Exeter and Plymouth.

Across the Irish Sea circles with recumbent stones, known there as 'multiple rings', were raised in south-west Ireland, the tallest stones positioned not alongside but opposite the recumbent. Many of them are still in good condition, protected by the superstition that to disturb the stones would be to invoke ill fortune. Some of them have white centre stones like those in Cornwall, 200 miles (320 km) away across the waters travelled by early prospectors in search of copper, gold and tin. Further inland, deep in the Boggeragh mountains, even tinier five-stone rings

34. Drombeg, County Cork, a good example of an Irish recumbent ('multiple') stone circle.

six from the intervening ring-cairn and ten from the indeterminate Newton of Petty suggested a construction for many of no earlier than about 1750 BC in calendar years, continuing down to a very late, even improbable, 950 BC. It now seems that these fine sites, with their surrounding stone circles graded in height towards the south-west, were not the ancestors of but successors to the recumbent stone circles of north-eastern Scotland.

There is no firm proof that any stone circle was built after 1500 BC. A deterioration in the climate caused the abandonment of many upland rings, and changes in religious belief may have led to the neglect of others. The latest known date for any circle is a C-14 assay of 970±60 bc, a wide period from about 1200 to 1070 BC, for a secondary and much later burial inside Cashelkeety West, a five-stone ring in County Kerry. And that ring, too, was shortly deserted to the rains and the growing peat.

7
Stonehenge: *c*.3000–1500 BC

Stonehenge was unlike any other stone circle. It was also in the wrong place. Salisbury Plain had few boulders, only forests and timber. The great ring was wood translated into sandstone. The nearest stone-built chambered tomb was over 14 miles (23 km) away at Tisbury and Fosbury not far from the sarsens of the Marlborough Downs. In 2500 BC Stonehenge was not a typical stone circle but a representation in enduring stone of a timber building that had been erected on the site five centuries earlier

This may have been a roofed mortuary house, almost 30 metres across, in which the dead were laid until their dried bones could be removed for burial in the neighbouring long barrows. The building had been erected inside the banks and inner ditch of an earthwork henge 98 metres in diameter. There was a narrow causeway at the exact south and a wider north-east entrance aligned on the midwinter moonrise. Beyond it the outlying Heel Stone marked the midpoint of the moon's 18.61 year lunar cycle from north-east to NNE and back again.

A century or two later burials were added. Twenty-five cremations have been recovered from the Aubrey Holes, a ring of fifty-six chalk-cut pits winding along the inner edge of the bank. Thirty other cremations lay in the ditch and near the bank, one of them with a lovely stone macehead of striped gneiss, perhaps from Brittany, perhaps Scotland,

38. A general view of Stonehenge from the south-west.

meticulously deposited in line with the southern moonrise.

Then, in the decades near 2700 BC, bluestones from the Preseli mountains of south-west Wales were put up in two concentric settings, either unfinished circles or, more probably, horseshoes, where the decayed and demolished timber building had stood. How the stones reached Salisbury Plain – whether by human transportation or by glaciation – remains contentious.

There was a dramatic change in ritual. Newcomers widened the north-eastern entrance so that its midpoint would frame the midsummer sun rising just to the left of the ancient Heel Stone. The alteration suggests a radical change from a lunar to a solar cult seemingly associated with users of native pottery.

Just inside the bank the short eastern and western sides of a rectangle of four stones known as the four Stations pointed to that sunrise, while the long sides were directed towards the most northerly setting of the moon. Entirely by coincidence Stonehenge had been built close to the latitude where these celestial events occurred at right angles to each other.

39. The circle at Stonehenge. In the foreground is Stone 93, a stunted survivor of the four Stations.

40. The carvings of axes and a dagger (indicated by an arrow) on Trilithon 53 at Stonehenge.

There was further astronomical ingenuity. Rather than a square, a rectangle had been chosen so that its ESE–WNW diagonal indicated the May Day sunset, an alignment that anticipated the so-called Iron Age 'Celtic' festival of Beltane by over two thousand years. It was a geometrical construction reminiscent of the Crucuno quadrilateral in southern Brittany.

There was disruption. The bluestones were uprooted and around 2500 BC heavy blocks of sarsen were laboriously manhandled from the Marlborough Downs 20 miles (32 km) to the north. Five towering archways known as trilithons were set up inside the lintelled circle of sarsens, arranged in a horseshoe-shaped setting open to the north-east.

The bluestones were returned to form a rough circle inside the sarsen circle and a more elegant horseshoe inside the trilithons. The long Altar Stone was laid at the heart of the monument. Visual effect was everything. Despite the monument's apparent permanence it was an architectural disaster. Some stones had foundations that were dangerously insecure. Some were not long enough. Some were cracked. The result was an impressive but ramshackle edifice.

The native carpenters of Salisbury Plain had treated the monstrous sarsens as though they were wooden beams to be smoothed, rebated, chamfered, jointed by mortise and tenons and tongue-and-grooved, ring-beamed –

urn and a beaker were placed. Just to the north is a cupmarked outcrop, and to the south-east is a fallen cupmarked outlier.

Machrie Moor, Arran (plate 4). NR 912324. *2³/4 miles (4.5 km) north of Blackwaterfoot.*

   1 ¹/2 mile (2.5 km) walk. No fewer than seven different stone circles can be seen here, first a cairn circle at Moss Farm, then, half a mile (800 metres) further into the moor, a concentric, a possible four-poster, two plain rings, a horseshoe and a 'new' ring excavated in 1978. 1¹/4 miles (2 km) NNE is the Auchagallon variant recumbent stone circle (NR 893346).

Ménec West, Carnac, Morbihan, Brittany (plate 16).

   The best-preserved of the Breton cromlechs but difficult to see in its entirety because of houses built inside it. It is an egg-shaped ring, 91 by 71 metres, with good arcs of closely set stones at north-west, east and south. From the east twelve straggling rows of well-spaced stones lead to it. The most regular, the third and fourth from the road, may be the pillars of an original avenue 70 metres long. They are linked with the avenue from Ménec East. Wire meshing prevents a stroll down the lines.

Merry Maidens, Cornwall. SW 432245. *1¹/2 miles (2.5 km) south-east of St Buryan.*

   A lovely, almost perfect, plain ring with a possible east entrance. By the road downhill from the circle is the Tregiffian chambered tomb with a cupmarked entrance.

Pobull Fhinn, North Uist, Outer Hebrides. NF 844650. *5 miles (8 km) WSW of Lochmaddy.*

   Perhaps in the loveliest setting of all stone circles — in good weather! — this large and irregular ring overlooks a countryside of lochs and moorland. With possible entrances at east and west, the stones stand in a bank on an artificially levelled terrace.

Rollright Stones, Oxfordshire (plate 24). SP 296308. *2¹/2 miles (4 km) north-west of Chipping Norton.*

   A circle of ragged limestones has a portal dolmen, the Whispering Knights, in the field to its east and an outlying pillar, the King Stone, to its NNE. Legends of witchcraft are associated with this attractive ring.

St-Just, Ille-et-Vilaine, Brittany. *6¹/4 miles (10 km) east of La Gacilly. Along a bumpy track west of the village.*

   There is a megalithic wonderland here of the two rows of the 'Alignements du Moulin'; the Château-Bu, a Scottish four-poster on top of a passage-tomb; a small cromlech and other intriguing sites.

Sanctuary, Wiltshire. SU 118679. *5 miles (8 km) west of Marlborough.*

No stone survives of this important ring, destroyed in 1724. Despite the ugly concrete blocks and pillars that represent its lost stones and posts, it is worth a visit for its association with Avebury and the Kennet Avenue. Two concentric stone circles succeeded several timber structures, one of which may have been a Neolithic mortuary chamber. The site lies by the prehistoric Ridgeway near several Bronze Age round barrows.

Stanton Drew, Somerset (plate 20). ST 603630. *6 miles (9.5 km) south of Bristol.*

A great stone circle about 110 metres in diameter is flanked by the remains of two smaller rings Two ruined avenues led down to the river Chew. In line with the north-east and central rings a cove stands behind the church near the Druid's Arms. *Charge requested.*

Stenness, Orkney (plate 14). HY 306125. *4 miles (6.5 km) ENE of Stromness.*

Only four stones survive of this large circle-henge with its rock-cut ditch. Three of them are at least 4.6 metres high. A version of a cove stands near the middle.

Stonehenge, Wiltshire (plates 2, 38, 39 and 40). SU 123422. *2 miles (3.2 km) west of Amesbury.*

A simple henge, *c*.3000 BC, was succeeded by a possible concentric bluestone horseshoe, *c*.2700 BC, which in turn was replaced by the well-known sarsen circle, *c*.2500 BC, with its imposing horseshoe of trilithons. Two of the four Stations rectangle that preceded the ring survive. The outlying Heel Stone stands alongside the A344. One may now walk across the plain from the east end of the Cursus, a Neolithic earthwork (SU 137434), and along the avenue that led to the henge's north-east entrance. It is not possible to enter the roped-off ring but one may walk around it. *Charge.*

Sunhoney, Aberdeenshire. NJ 716058. *1¹/₂ miles (2.5 km) east of Echt.*

This fine recumbent stone circle, its stones set in a rubble bank, has a superbly cupmarked recumbent. Cremated bone was found in 1865. The recumbent stone circle of Midmar Kirk is 1 mile (1.5 km) to the WNW. Both recumbents are in line with the minor southern moonset.

Swinside, Cumbria (plate 11). SD 172883. *2¹/₂ miles (4 km) ENE of Broughton-in-Furness.*

³/₄ mile (1 km) walk. A very attractive, large circle. It has a tall north stone and a south-east entrance of double portal stones. Excavation in 1901 found only charcoal and decayed bone.

Temple Wood, Argyll (plate 41). NR 827979. *6¹/₂ miles (10.5 km) NNW of Lochgilphead.*

This circle stands in the Kilmartin Valley with its standing stones, cairns and decorated cist slabs. Excavations in 1928–9 and 1974 onwards proved the ring to have been oval. It was later converted into a ring-cairn by the addition of dry-stone walling. Internal cists contained cremations. A double spiral was carved on the north stone. A second circle was discovered to the north.

Torhousekie, Wigtownshire. NX 383565. *3¹/₂ miles (5.5 km) WNW of Wigtown.*
   This variant recumbent stone circle has stones graded in height towards the south-east and a 'recumbent' and its flankers inside the ring. 120 metres to the east is a three-stone row.

Tossen-Keler, Penvenan, Côte-de-Nord, Brittany.
   A fine moved and re-erected horseshoe. From the small town centre, a short walk down the hill to the harbour. Shrubs have been planted within the fifty-eight stones. The *fer-à-cheval* faces east and is 29 metres long.

Tregeseal, Cornwall (plate 1). SW 387324. *1¹/₂ miles (2.5 km) north-east of St Just.*
   This well-preserved ring is the eastern survivor of a pair of circles. Originally nineteen tall stones stood on the circumference of a flattened circle about 22 metres in diameter.

Trippet Stones, Cornwall. SX 131750. *6 miles (9.5 km) north-east of Bodmin.*
   A pleasing ring once of about twenty-six stones in a true circle 33 metres across. The Stripple Stones circle-henge, SX 144752, can be seen uphill half a mile (800 metres) to the north-east.

10
Further reading

Aubrey, J. *Monumenta Britannica, I, II* (1665–93). Dorset Publishing Company, 1980, 1982.

Barnatt, J. *Stone Circles of Britain, I, II*. British Archaeological Reports 215, 1989.

Barnatt, J. *The Henges, Stone Circles and Ring-cairns of the Peak District*. University of Sheffield, 1990.

Burgess, C. *The Age of Stonehenge*. J. M. Dent, 2001.

Burl, A. *Prehistoric Avebury*. Yale University Press, 1979.

Burl, A. *Megalithic Brittany: A Guide to Over 350 Sites and Monuments*. Thames & Hudson, 1985.

Burl, A. *The Stonehenge People*. J. M. Dent, 1987.

Burl, A. *From Carnac to Callanish: The Prehistoric Avenues and Rows of Britain, Ireland and Brittany*. Yale University Press, 1993.

Burl, A. *A Guide to the Stone Circles of Britain, Ireland and Brittany*. Yale University Press, 1995.

Burl, A. *Great Stone Circles*. Yale University Press, 1999.

Burl, A. *The Stone Circles of Britain, Ireland and Brittany*. Yale University Press, 2000.

Burl, A. *Prehistoric Astronomy and Ritual*. Shire Publications, second edition 2005.

Castleden, R. *The Making of Stonehenge*. Routledge, 1993.

Chippindale, C. *Stonehenge Complete*. Thames & Hudson, 2004.

Cleal, R. M. J.; Walker, K. E.; and Montague, R. (editors). *Stonehenge in Its Landscape*. English Heritage, 1995.

Cope, J. *The Modern Antiquarian: A Pre-Millennium Odyssey through Megalithic Britain, Including a Gazetteer to over 300 Prehistoric Sites*. Thorsons, 1998.

Cope, J. *The Megalithic European. The 21st Century Traveller in Prehistoric Europe*. Element, 2004.

Darvill, T. *Prehistoric Britain*. Batsford, 1987.

Gibson, A. *Stonehenge and Timber Monuments*. Tempus, 1998.

Heggie, D. C. *Megalithic Science*. Thames & Hudson, 1981.

Lockyer, Sir N. *Stonehenge and Other British Stone Monuments Astronomically Considered*. Macmillan, second edition 1909.

MacKie, E. W. *Science and Society in Prehistoric Britain*. Elek, 1977.

O'Nuallain, S. *Stone Circles in Ireland*. Town and Country House, 1995.

Pitts, M. *Hengeworld*. Century, 2000.

Ponting, G. and M. *New Light on the Stones of Callanish*. G. and M. Ponting, 1984.

Ruggles, C. L. N. *Astronomy in Prehistoric Britain and Ireland*. Yale University Press, 1999.

Thom, A. *Megalithic Sites in Britain*. Oxford University Press, 1967.

Thom, A. and A. S. *Megalithic Remains in Britain and Brittany*. Oxford University Press, 1978.

Thom, A. and A. S., and Burl, A. *Megalithic Rings: Plans and Data for 229 Sites*. British Archaeological Reports, 81, 1980.

Twohig, E. S. *The Megalithic Art of Western Europe*. Clarendon Press, 1981.

Waterhouse, J. *The Stone Circles of Cumbria*. Phillimore, 1985.

64

Index

Page numbers in bold type are important references; those in italic refer to photographs.